Entomology

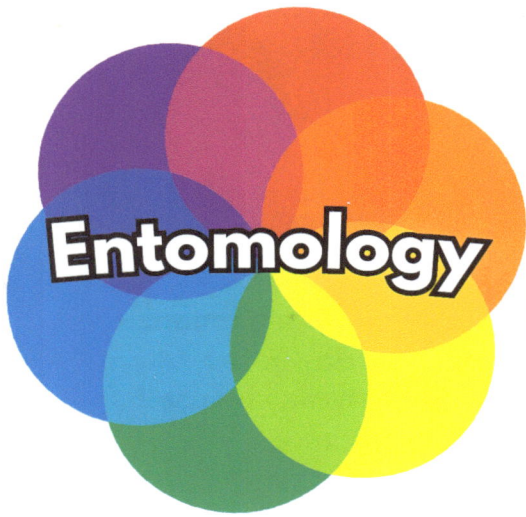

Book of COLORS

A Rainbow of Insects

AO PRESS

Jessica Lee Anderson

Paperback ISBN: 978-1-964078-40-3

To Crystal McGough, a fan of nature and insects too! Thanks for all of your support! - JLA

Insects are often multi-colored, so have fun pointing out the variety of colors in addition to the featured colors. The photos are not to scale.

Photo credits, left to right, top to bottom: Front cover: Egor Kamelev (Leaf beetle); Interior cover: Somrek Kossolwitthayanant (Jewel Beetle); Copyright page: (Ladybug): Ale-ks; Dedication page: aukidphumsirichat, nickjamesstock, Backyard Productions, camacho9999, Aldolphew, Billion Photos; p. 4: Egor Kamelev, Cabezonification, Vinicius Souza; p. 5: Pcha988, Canoneer, cwk15; p. 6: ineb1599, Sheila Brown, gstalker; p. 7: membio, Amit Rane, Christopher Kimball; p. 8: Dimijana, Edward Snow, Trevor Meunier; p. 9: Antony Cooper, Ken Wiedemann, Warren Farnell; p. 10: LWO Photography, Rejean Bedard, Cal Dezign; p. 11: Desi Aryanti, Ines Carrara, Joseph Accurso; p. 12: mirceax, Suwat Sirivutcharungc, Phil Mitchell; p. 13: IJPHoto, Christina_Aniballi_Krinaphoto, bookguy; p. 14: Vitalii Hulai, marcouliana, nomis_g; p. 15: Hana Richterova, lnzyxs, Duncan McCulloch; p. 16: ktreffinger, Thirawatana Phaisalratana, chris2766; p. 17: webguzs, Wes Harrison, quangpraha; p. 18: Khlongwangchao, gyro, Ines Carrara; p. 19: Life On White, Four Oaks, Joa_Souza; p. 20: yuelan, Nur Diana, Vinisouza128; p. 21: dgfoto, Frank Ramspott, Tomasz Klejdysz; p. 22: Ian_Redding, Holly Guerrio, xalanx; p. 23: Heather Broccard-Bell, TommyIX, Edward Snow; p. 24: Klein, Kevin Dyer, Vinicius Souza; p. 25: Science Photo Library, Vinícius Rodrigues de Souza, idmanjoe; p. 26: Victor Njoroge, nicosmit, Dopeyden; p. 27: Prasenjit Malakar, BethWolff43, sdewitt92; p. 28: manfredxy, Patrick_Gijsbers, blightlylad-infocus; p. 29: Tom Brakefield, Ritesh Ghosh, cturtletrax; 30: Kathy Keifer, Jose Michael Murillo Rojas, Wirestock; p. 31: Ines Carrara (top row), Erik Agar; p. 32: Stephane Bidouze, lukasjonaitis, Rhagu Ramaswamy; p. 33: milehightraveler, Prasit Supho, Desi Aryanti; p. 34: Michael Anderson; Back cover (Jewel beetle): Somrek Kosolwitthayanant

This Book Belongs to:

_____

Blow fly

Firefly

Velvet ant

Fire ant

Entomology is the study of insects.

Rainbow grasshopper

Stag beetle

Red

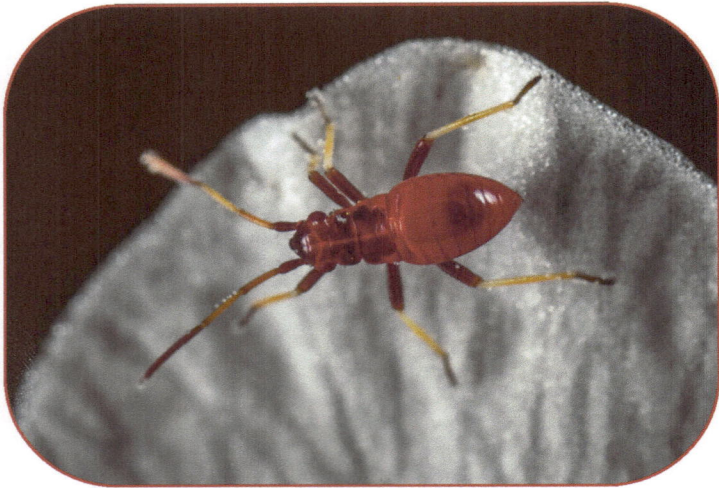

Red assassin bug

Red ants

Adult insects have three pairs of legs, three body segments, and antennae.

Spotless lady beetle

4

Red

Red paper wasp

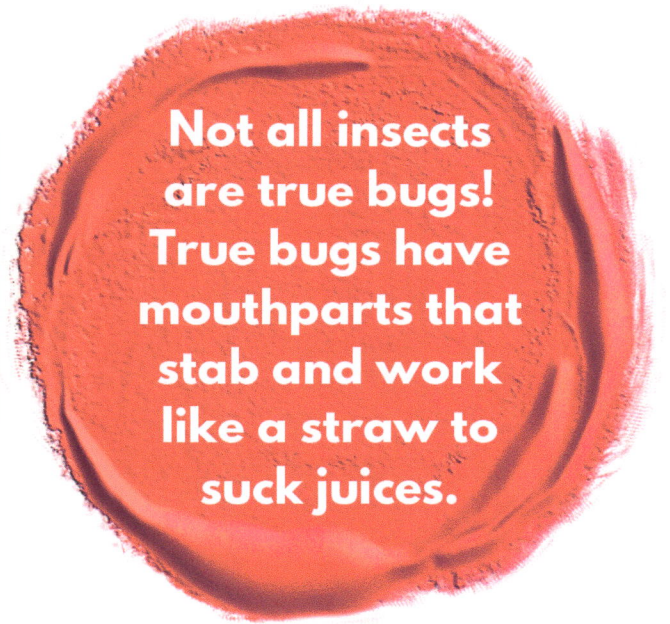

Not all insects are true bugs! True bugs have mouthparts that stab and work like a straw to suck juices.

Autumn meadowhawk dragonfly

Cardinal beetle

Orange

Cloudless sulfur butterfly

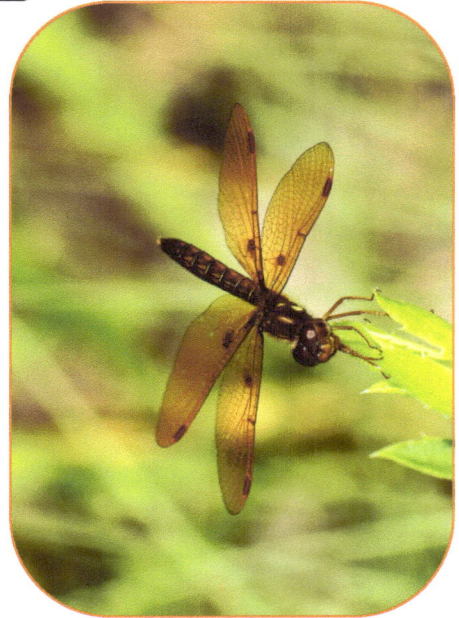
Eastern amber wing dragonfly

Insects have a hard covering on the outside of their bodies called an exoskeleton.

Net-winged beetle

Orange

Short-horned grasshopper

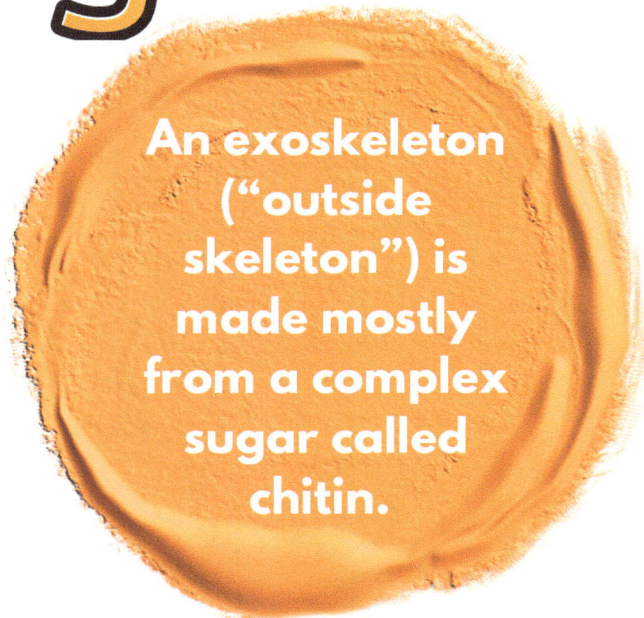

An exoskeleton ("outside skeleton") is made mostly from a complex sugar called chitin.

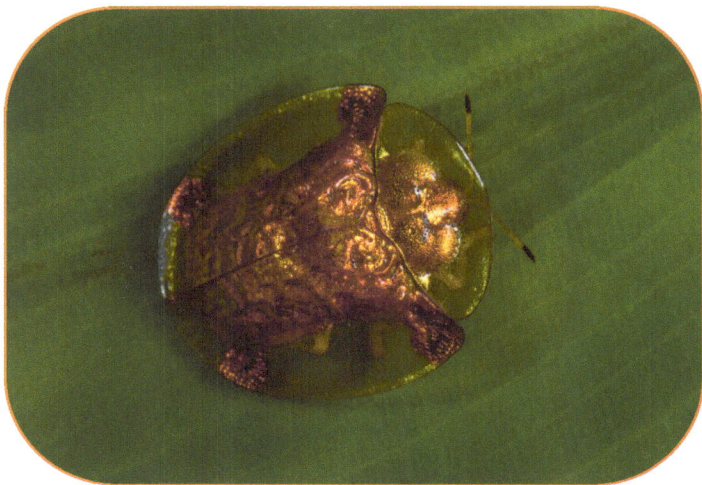

Tortoise beetle

Fiery skipper butterfly

Yellow

Milkweed aphids

Eastern Hercules beetle

Insects range in size from smaller than a freckle to longer than your hand.

Jagged ambush bug

Yellow

Yellow jacket

Almost all adult insects have wings. Many insect species can fly long distances!

Yellow woolly bear caterpillar

Dung fly

Green

Stink bug

Katydid

Insects have heads with eyes, mouths, and antennae.

Leaf insect

Green

Cuckoo wasp

Antennae help insects detect smell, touch, motion, and even taste!

Lacewing

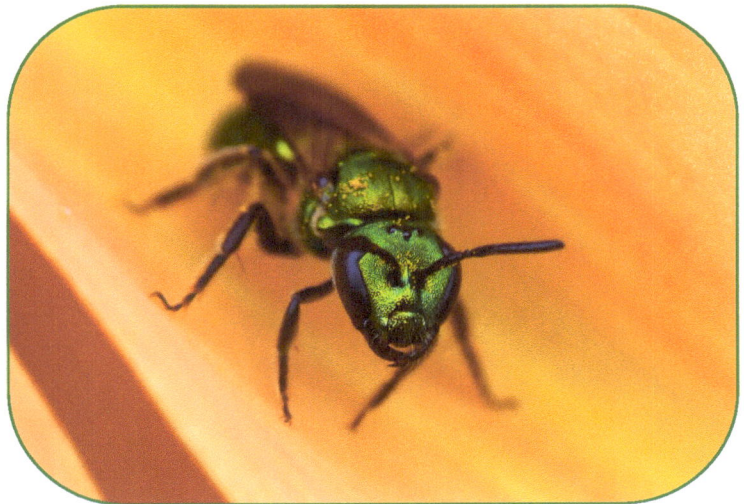

Sweat bee

Blue

The middle part of an insect is called the thorax. This is where an insect's wings and six legs are attached.

Blue mud dauber

Frog-legged leaf beetle

Blue bottle fly

Blue

Alder leaf beetle

Damselfly

Blue dasher dragonfly

The abdomen is located behind the thorax. It houses organs for digestion and reproduction.

Purple

Diving beetle

Purple flower beetle

There are around one million species of insects that scientists are aware of!

Violet dropwing dragonfly

Purple

Violet ground beetle

Scientists are continuing to learn more about insects and discover new species.

Purple leaf beetle

Bereft snail-eating beetle

15

Pink

Roseate skimmer dragonfly

Orchid mantis

Bright colors can help insects attract mates, blend in, or to warn predators they might be harmful.

Pink grasshopper

Pink

False leaf katydid

Some insect species are social and gather in swarms or live together in groups called colonies.

Oblong-winged katydid

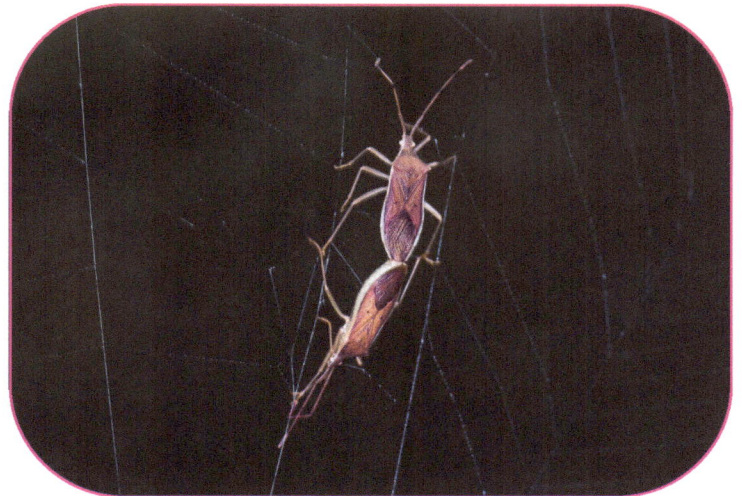

Pink assassin bugs

Black

Giraffe stag beetle

Emma field cricket

Many insects dine on plants and fruits. Some sip nectar while others drink blood.

Black bumbebee

Black

Black carpenter ants

Decomposer insects keep ecosystems healthy by eating dead plants and animals. Some even eat poop!

Dung beetles

Rhinoceros beetle

White

Silk moth

Laugher caterpillar

A baby insect is called a larva or a nymph depending on how it will grow and develop.

White scale insect (with ant)

White

Mayfly

Insects live in almost every habitat on Earth, from scorching hot deserts to snowy mountains.

Woolly beech aphid

Greenhouse whitefly

Gray

Earl grey moth

Little leaf notcher weevil

Insects have been around since ancient times. Research has shown that they existed before dinosaurs!

Longhorn beetle

Gray

Silverfish

Insects often blend into their environment (camouflage) to avoid predators or ambush prey.

Bark mantis

Thistledown velvet ant

Brown

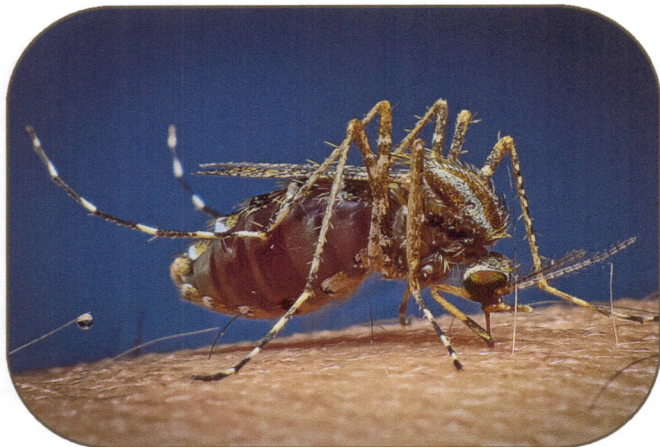

Mosquito

Head lice

A few insects can carry disease or cause discomfort. Insects, even pests, are an important source of food for a variety of animals.

American cockroach

Brown

Honey bee

Certain insects pollinate plants, helping produce fruits and seeds. A small number of bee species produce sweet honey!

Common earwig

Stick insect

COLOR Combinations

Can you describe the colors and patterns of these insects?

Green milkweed locust

Gaudy grasshopper

Barber pole grasshopper

COLOR Combinations

Carpenter bee

Cairns birdwing butterfly

Hummingbird moth

What do you notice about the shapes, colors, and features of these flying insects?

COLOR Combinations

What are some colors and patterns you notice?

Fire bug

Stink bugs

Pharaoh cicada

COLOR Combinations

Thorn bugs (treehoppers)

Thorn-hopper

Thorn bugs (treehoppers)

How might colors, shapes, and patterns help these treehoppers survive?

29

COLOR Combinations

Can you describe the colors, patterns, and features of these mantises?

Spiny mantis

Peruvian shield mantis

Iris mantis

COLOR Combinations

Yellow ladybug

Striped ladybug

Spotted pink ladybeetle

What are some things you notice about the shapes, colors, and features of these beetles?

COLOR Combinations

Can you describe these insect colors and patterns?

Blue jewel bug

Leaf rolling weevil

Tiger beetle

COLOR Combinations

Giraffe-necked weevil

Lantern fly

Stalk-eyed fly

Why do you think the colors, shapes, and features of an insect matters?

Jessica Lee Anderson is an award-winning author of over 75 books for young readers including the NAOMI NASH chapter book series. Jessica loves spending time in nature and exploring the outdoors with her husband, Michael, and their daughter, Ava! Jessica loves admiring insects (especially butterflies) near her home in Austin, Texas. You can learn more about Jessica by visiting www.jessicaleeanderson.com.

Check out these other books:

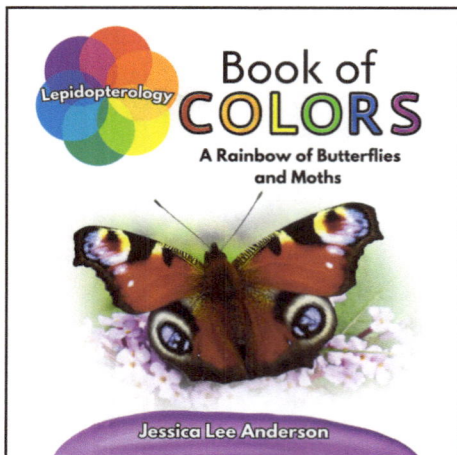

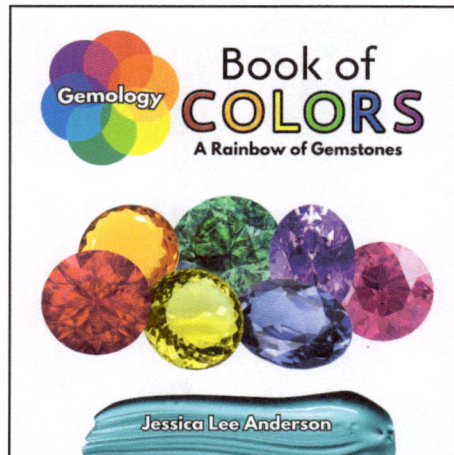

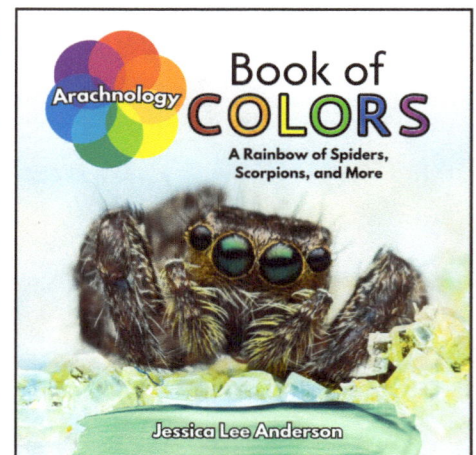

Lepidopterology
Book of COLORS
A Rainbow of Butterflies and Moths
Jessica Lee Anderson

Gemology
Book of COLORS
A Rainbow of Gemstones
Jessica Lee Anderson

Arachnology
Book of COLORS
A Rainbow of Spiders, Scorpions, and More
Jessica Lee Anderson

www.ingramcontent.com/pod-product-compliance
Lightning Source LLC
Chambersburg PA
CBHW061144030426
42335CB00002B/97

9 781964 078403